D1826630

Church
Organs

CIO PUBLISHING
Dean's Yard, London SW1P 3NZ

ISBN 0 7151 7547 5

Published 1985 by CIO Publishing for the Council for the Care of Churches and prepared by the Organs Advisory Committee of the Council for the Care of Churches in association with the Royal School of Church Music

Printed in England by Tasprint Ltd.

CONTENTS

I INTRODUCTION

The object of this booklet is to provide basic information about church organs with practical guidance on their provision, maintenance and alteration. Intended primarily for Church of England parishes, it may also be helpful to Diocesan Advisory Committees and to churches of other denominations. It also states the general policy upon these particular matters of the Organs Advisory Committee.

The Organs Advisory Committee is a sub-committee of the Council for the Care of Churches, a permanent commission of the General Synod of the Church of England with offices at 83 London Wall, London EC2M 5NA (01-638 0971), which provides advice on all aspects of the care of churches and their contents and co-ordinates the work of the Diocesan Advisory Committees. The Committee's membership covers a wide range of knowledge and experience in all aspects of organs, including their musical quality, construction, appearance and history. Its duty is primarily discharged by this booklet, supplemented by occasional leaflets on such subjects as electronic organs or the agreed policy of Diocesan Organs Advisers.

The Committee organises annual conferences for Diocesan Organs Advisers, at which they can keep abreast of development in the field of organ building and restoration by hearing papers, visiting organs both historic and contemporary, and by sharing experience in discussion. It has a particular interest in historic organs, upon which it is always pleased to advise. In certain circumstances grants towards the restoration of such organs may be offered from funds provided annually by the Pilgrim Trust and other charitable bodies (see Section XII). Enquiries addressed to the Clerk to the Committee will be answered by reference either to Committee members or to the Council's library and national survey of churches. The library includes a section on church music and organs, and is available for use by researchers by prior appointment.

II PARISH CHURCH REQUIREMENTS

There are many musical instruments whose design varies according to musical function, but none so much as the organ. Obviously organs differ widely in appearance, size and tonal power, but these are by no means the only matters of variation. Much depends on the availability and disposition of stops (see Section III under 'Size and Tonal Design'),

1

so that an organ designed specifically for music of a particular historical period may be utterly unsuitable for another; and the capacity to deal satisfactorily with many different musical styles in solo performance will not necessarily imply equal suitability for church service accompaniment. We have therefore to state categorically that *the primary purpose of a parish church organ is liturgical accompaniment.* Its design should be directed to that end.

In order of importance the specific functions of a parish church organ may be listed as follows:

(a) Leading and sustaining congregational singing.

(b) Accompanying the church choir.

(c) Solo performance of organ music in a liturgical context (e.g. voluntaries, and enhancing the moods of worship by inducing, for example, an atmosphere of repose or joyful celebration).

To these may be added as liturgically inessential but desirable according to local circumstances:

(d) The demands of local musical events such as organ recitals, continuo work and choral society accompaniment.

The problems facing parishes in providing for these requirements are largely inter-related, but conveniently considered under a number of separate headings.

III BASIC INFORMATION ABOUT ORGANS

Siting The Organ

Principles of Good Siting

The musical effect of an organ is largely dependent upon its siting. Not even the best voicing and tonal design can overcome a poor position. A well-placed church organ will meet four basic requirements. First, like any other musical instrument it should be a free-standing entity openly placed in the building. Secondly, organ pipes should speak freely and without impediment to the egress of sound. For ideal results the various divisions should be disposed either vertically or side-by-side (an arrangement known technically as the *Werkprinzip*). But if, for example, they are arranged on the same level behind each other under a low ceiling or chamber roof, the tonal results will be stifled and musically unsatisfying. Thirdly, the organ, organist and choir should all be together and within reasonable distance of the congregation. It is both difficult and discouraging for choirs and congregations to sing at any appreciable distance from the accompanying instrument. Lastly and by no means least, the organ should be architecturally harmonious, i.e. it should be clad in casework of artistically competent design, and its siting should not give rise to any of the faults mentioned immediately below.

Positions to be Avoided

It is an unfortunate fact that many English church organs are poorly sited, for reasons inherited from the last 150 years. During the two centuries or so following the Restoration of the Monarchy in 1660 the common site of a parish church organ – where one could be afforded – was the west gallery. But fairly soon in the Victorian era parish churches began to adopt the arrangements of cathedrals where quires had been opened up by the removal of stone screens. Choir stalls and robed choristers were introduced into narrow chancels; and to accompany the choirs organs were moved eastwards and re-erected, often considerably enlarged, in restricted chancel or side chapel positions they were never meant to occupy. Organs introduced into previously organ-less churches were given similarly unsatisfactory positions. Often lack of space brought about the purpose-built organ chamber, from which the sound had to percolate into the body of the church as best it could.

It is easy to see where an organ should not be. In a mediaeval building it should never interfere with the line of the chancel, second in importance only to the sanctuary. It should not spoil the proportions of a cruciform building by occupying an entire transept; nor should it upset the balance of an aisle by filling an east end originally intended for a side chapel. The visual damage is worsened if the organ lacks casework or has visible woodwork finished to a tone out of keeping with other woodwork in the building. Transept sites are open to the further objection of causing a concentration of sound at the crossing and giving insufficient support to the people in the nave. They may also be too far from a chancel choir. The internal proportions of a classical building can be ruined by a former west gallery organ re-erected at the eastern end of a side gallery or an aisle. A musically effective chamber-sited organ is seldom found. There is virtually no chance of musically acceptable results unless the chamber is spacious in relation to the size of the instrument 'and freely connected to the church.

Fortunately, recent advances in organ design have reduced floor area requirements to a degree of compactness that should make it unnecessary to resort to undesirable locations, especially if the organ is not too large. Indeed, siting difficulties are often exacerbated by the organ being larger than is really necessary. Many churches have no space for an organ of any but a very modest size, and unless this fact is accepted a satisfactory solution is rarely possible.

West End Sites

Siting the organ and choir in a west gallery can be an excellent arrangement if it is possible without architectural detriment. Organs placed above and behind the congregation tend to have an encouraging effect upon ·singing, and a small organ in such a position can be exceptionally effective in relation to its size. The musical effect may also be enhanced by the sound-reflecting property of a west wall. Nevertheless an open layout is just as important in a western position as elsewhere — a cramped tower arch site can be as bad as an organ chamber.

A west end position is most suited to Georgian churches which were frequently designed for a west end organ and choir on a gallery. It is less suited to Gothic churches, especially where the nave is long or has a west window or tower arch that should not be obscured (unless it is proposed to reduce the seating in an overlarge building by forming a narthex, hall or vestries at the western end).

A west end organ with a chancel choir is a most unsatisfactory arrangement. Acoustic time lag will make unanimity extremely difficult, if not impossible, and the problem is not solved by providing a detached console with the choir. It is also unsatisfactory for the congregation to be sandwiched between the choir and the accompanying instrument, since the balance of power will vary according to the position of the listener.

Divided Organs

Where a west window precludes a central organ position, division of the organ may be expedient. Choir and console may then be placed between the divisions; but regard should be had to the effect of the sun's heat through large windows affecting one part of the organ and disturbing its tuning unequally. It may also be expedient for large organs in other positions to be divided, but this is rarely to the advantage of the instrument unless the alternative is overcrowding. A practical disadvantage of division is that the cost of organ and casework will be increased, likewise the difficulty of providing a responsive action.

Position of Console

Some organists regard a detached console as a first requirement. This is quite mistaken. Distance of detachment, unless very short, involves audible time lag; and for good organ playing, demanding precision of articulation and phrasing, the organist needs to be completely at one with his instrument. A detached console may be expedient on rare occasions where the only alternative is to place the organist where he cannot hear choir and congregation in reasonable balance, but the distance of detachment should be minimal. The tolerable maximum is 39 feet, beyond which time lag will make good organ playing virtually impossible. Detachment of more than about 10 feet will make it impractical to employ tracker action (see 'Types of Action').

Size and Tonal Design

The position of an organ is closely related to its bulk. This in turn is determined by the tonal design.

Tonal design is essentially the choice and disposition of the stops of an organ according to its function. The best organ building skills will be of little avail if the stop list (or 'specification') is wrong. Drawing up an organ specification is a specialist task calling for experience of many different organs, a sound knowledge of organ building principles, and a wide musical background. It should not be left to the parish organist, though his day-to-day knowledge of the effectiveness of an existing organ may well form a valuable contribution.

The first priority is to ensure that the chorus structure of the organ is as complete as possible. Even the smallest church organ should have a minimal chorus, because this constitutes the greatest asset of the instrument in the primary function of leading and sustaining congregational singing. No other instrument or instrumental ensemble can do this so well. The reason is simple. If the voices are led by unison pitches only, these must be unmusically loud to make any impression on the singers. On the other hand, the higher chorus pitches sing clearly and naturally above the voices without need for excessive power and can lead them without difficulty.

Many parish church organs are too large for their function and position. They are consequently economically wasteful and often far less useful than they would be if properly planned. A village church seating perhaps up to 150 people will be adequately served by a one-manual organ of three stops voiced as a chorus:

Stopped Diapason	8ft
Principal	4ft
Fifteenth	2ft

For slightly larger buildings, this might be supplemented by an Open Diapason 8ft, or a Mixture, or both. (It is not widely realised how much good organ music can be played satisfactorily on an organ of such modest proportions.) An enclosed division is by no means essential and may even be undesirable if the organist is unskilled. The same applies to pedal stops, but there is much to be said for providing a pedal board permanently coupled to the manual. The cost need not be great and an organist who wants to improve his technique would be provided with the essential equipment.

Larger organs will be needed according to the capacity of the building, the competence of the choir and the skill of the organist. In churches of medium size where there is a competent organist, a pedal organ and a second enclosed division (a 'Swell organ') are desirable. A building seating about 300 persons can be adequately served by a two-manual and pedal organ of 10 or 12 speaking stops. Normally a third manual is something of a luxury. Only in large churches where the music approaches cathedral standards can a sizeable three- or four-manual instrument be justified, provided architectural considerations allow. Even then a well-designed organ of about 35 speaking stops (three manuals and pedals) should be adequate for all accompanimental and solo purposes.

Types of Action

In this context 'action' means the mechanical connection between keys and pipes. Three types are commonly found today: tracker, tubular-pneumatic and electric. In tracker action – the oldest and simplest of all the types – there is a direct mechanical connection extending from the key to the 'pallet' (the valve which is pulled down to admit wind to the pipe). The other two types are more complicated and the direct mechanical connection is absent. In tubular-pneumatic action the connection is a stream of air in a tube – one for each note. In electric action the key serves as a switch to complete a circuit and energize an electro-magnet which, in turn, sets in motion the pipe-opening mechanism. Tubular pneumatic action is obsolete and no longer commercially available – which does not mean that it is necessarily inefficient or incapable of repair.

Not so very long ago tracker action was widely regarded as crude and obsolete. It has now returned to favour. Leading organists and organ builders throughout the world are agreed that under suitable working conditions it is superior to all other actions, for the following reasons:

(a) The direct mechanical connection provides instantaneous response. With appropriate voicing it enables a sensitivity of control over the attack and release of the pipe sound which no other action can approach, and consequently greater refinement of phrasing and articulation.

(b) It will last considerably longer than any other type of action and require less attention.

(c) Design advances in recent years have greatly reduced touch weight, even on quite large instruments.

The provision or retention of tracker action is therefore strongly recommended, wherever the physical circumstances are conducive to its efficient functioning.

Appearance and Casework

An organ should be one of the most beautiful of church furnishings, as pleasing to the eye as to the ear. An unclad organ is unavoidably unsightly, a defect which is not mitigated by attempts to arrange the visible parts more attractively. To be visually pleasing an organ must be clothed in a well-designed case. An organ case may be defined as a wooden structure enclosing the sides, back and sometimes the top of the instrument, the front of which is filled with decoratively arranged pipes and woodwork. Its purpose is not only decorative but also protective and, if so designed, tonal – i.e. the surrounding casework serves additionally as a resonating body enhancing the sound of the pipes. It should not be regarded as an avoidable expense. The protective qualities and tonal enhancement of a well-designed case make it an investment reducing servicing costs and promoting the historic value of the instrument. An unclad rack of pipes, however arranged and supported, is not an organ case. The presence of such displays in so many churches is one of the least attractive heritages from the mid-nineteenth century.

Organ case design is a highly specialised art calling for wide experience, creative skill and the application of design principles common to good organ cases of all styles and periods. It is a skill not possessed by all architects or master organ builders. Since even a limited treatment of the subject is beyond the scope of this booklet, readers desiring further knowledge of this extremely important aspect of the church organ are invited to consult the standard works mentioned in Appendix B or to seek advice from the Committee.

IV PROBLEMS OF EXISTING ORGANS

The problem most commonly faced is that of an old organ which is becoming unusable (though statements to this effect should be critically examined). The organ should be inspected by an independent and financially disinterested party – preferably the Diocesan Organs Adviser – with regard to its condition, artistic merit, historic importance and any work considered necessary. The DOA should advise the parish about the best method of obtaining tenders. The undermentioned courses are usually open:

1. *To repair or restore the organ as it stands*
This covers the majority of instances and, unless the organ is much too large or very badly sited, is usually the wisest and cheapest solution. The old organ may not be exactly what one would choose today, but it has probably served its purpose satisfactorily for many years and may well continue to do so indefinitely if thoroughly repaired. It is worth pondering whether any questions currently being raised as to the organ's suitability were not seriously discussed and resolved when it was originally provided. Renovation of an existing action, whatever the type, is normally preferable to replacement. It is essential to check that the organ builder is competent to deal with the type of action concerned. Organs of historic interest fall within a special category calling for special skills and experience (see Section XII).

2. *To repair it with some tonal alterations*
Old organs of no special artistic merit may be conspicuously improved by minor tonal adjustments such as a modest brightening of the chorus or the substitution of a chorus stop for one of lesser utility. Any additions should be in sympathy with the tonal character of the instrument and match it in pipe material, scaling and voicing method. A warning must be given against organists' 'pipe dreams' such as a radical enlargement of the specification, console gadgetry and alterations not strictly necessitated by liturgical requirements.

3. *To replace it by a new pipe organ*
If an existing organ is of low artistic merit and too large for present needs, and the cost of repairs seems disproportionately high, then it may make better sense to spend the equivalent (or perhaps a lesser sum) on replacing it by a new and smaller organ of superior design and appearance. Such a step should not be undertaken lightly and certainly not without the best possible advice. In any event, care should be taken to ensure that the tonal design of a new instrument is determined strictly by liturgical needs.

4. *To replace it by a secondhand pipe organ*
A secondhand pipe organ may provide a good alternative replacement where a new organ cannot be afforded, though it may be difficult to

find one of the right size and shape. Parishes who wish to explore this possibility might consider consulting the Redundant Organs Officer of the British Institute of Organ Studies (see Appendix A), who keeps a list of worthy organs in need of new homes. They should nevertheless bear in mind that to an attractively low initial price must be added the costs of dismantling, moving and re-erection, and probably of cleaning and overhauling. The total expense may well approach, even exceed, that of a new organ.

5. *To rebuild it elsewhere in the church*
The liturgical re-ordering of a church may suggest the removal of the choir to another part of the building and the consequent re-siting of the organ. In that event the alternative possibilities mentioned under 'Siting the Organ' will invite consideration. Nevertheless:

(a) Moving an organ – even a short distance – is a major operation involving the costly work of complete dismantling and reassembly on the new site.

(b) An organ designed for an organ chamber or a transept is unlikely to be visually suitable for an open site elsewhere. It will probably be too deep from back to front and the sides will be inadequately clad.

(c) While the tone of such an organ may be improved in an open position, it may be too strident if voiced for speech from a restricted chamber.

These factors and the cost of moving the organ may suggest replacement by a smaller and more compact instrument designed for the new position.

6. *To find an electronic substitute*
When an organ reaches the point where major expenditure is required, parishes may feel that they should investigate the alternative of an electronic instrument. Such instruments are extensively advertised in magazines and usually cost a fraction of the price of a new pipe organ with the same number of stop controls. They also require much less space than pipe organs with equivalent stop lists.

However, pipe organs continue to be made and, in an appreciable number of churches, have replaced electronic instruments. The reasons for this are threefold:

(a) The great majority of churches do not need an organ of anywhere near the size implied by the stop list of most electronic instruments. If this is taken into account the difference in space and cost is much reduced.

(b) Despite advances in technology, it is still necessary to make serious compromises in the design of commercial electronic instruments in order to minimise costs. The musical disadvantages which result are not always apparent at first hearing but primarily affect the leading of congregational singing. Competent and dedicated church musicians are in short supply; they will not be encouraged by the provision of instruments which are musically inferior.

(c) Electronic organs have been on the market for about 50 years now, a long enough period for experience to accumulate as to their practical life span. This varies widely between makes and is often governed by the availability of specialist spare parts. Instruments more than 20 years old are relatively uncommon.

Of course, only a minority of electronic organs are designed for churches. Most are designed for home entertainment, for the performance of non-liturgical music, and have a musical design loosely derived from the cinema organ. Their makers do not intend them to be capable of leading singing and they are not recommended in any circumstances. Instruments made specifically for church music can be suitable for outdoor rallies and other temporary situations where portability and high power are paramount. However, in view of their disadvantages, it is very rare for them to be recommended for fixed installations in churches. A new small pipe organ or the restoration of an existing one is normally much to be preferred.

More detailed information on this subject is available in a pamphlet *Electronic Organs* published by the Council for the Care of Churches.

V ORGANS FOR NEW CHURCHES

When designing a new church many architects are inadequately briefed and consequently do not make adequate provision for the organ. Too often the result is an insurmountable problem for the organ builder and an ineffective instrument. Consultation between the architect, the Diocesan Organs Adviser and a competent organ builder should take place well before the church designs have approached their final stage.

At the expense of some repetition we would stress:

(a) The organ should be free-standing, openly placed in the church. Organ chambers are unacceptable.

(b) It should be enclosed by a suitable case.

(c) Both organ and choir should be regarded as a single planning unit to be placed together, but with the organ as near to the congregation as possible.

A proposal to instal a secondhand organ in a new church should be examined with caution, since this implies that insufficient funds have been budgeted for in the musical allocation and that account may not have been taken of associated costs likely to be involved. The points mentioned under 'Secondhand Organs' apply with equal force.

VI HISTORIC ORGANS

An organ may be said to possess historical value if it is a good example of a past school of organ building in original or not substantially altered condition. For practical convenience this may be taken to mean organs built before c. 1900, but the division is necessarily arbitrary. Historic value may also subsist in other aspects of an organ such as casework, mechanism or historical association. Casework can be especially important if integral with an original instrument; but an antique case may outlast more than one instrument and accordingly possess historic value in its own right. Musicological interest apart, historic organs will almost invariably have proved their value as liturgical instruments over a long period of years. Parishes fortunate enough to possess one of these instruments are the trustees of an irreplaceable part of the national heritage, carrying with it the moral obligation to preserve and, where necessary, faithfully restore.

The repair or restoration of an historic organ calls for special skills and experience which not all organ builders possess. No work should be put in hand without advice from the Diocesan Organs Adviser and/or the Organs Advisory Committee. Restorations approved by the Committee may attract grants from funds at their disposal.

A parish whose organ was built before c. 1900 is therefore advised to establish whether it is of historic value. The area of interest has broadened so much in recent years that it is impractical to give here even a select list of makers; and in any event positive identification is an expert matter. The Organs Advisory Committee is willing to advise whenever possible. A select list of historic organs and organ cases in the British Isles is published in the Gazetteer to *The British Organ* by Cecil Clutton and Austin Niland (revised 2nd edition, 1982).

VII ADVICE

Diocesan Organs Advisers

Every Diocesan Advisory Committee includes amongst its number at least one Diocesan Organ Adviser who is also available to advise parishes. When contemplating work to the organ a parish should consult the Adviser at the earliest possible stage. He is an independent and financially disinterested party who can suggest ways in which the existing organ can best be treated, whether by restoration, improvement or replacement. He can also give advice on proposals received from organ builders and can warn the parish about matters which at first sight may appear unconnected with organs; the presence of thick hangings, the laying of large areas of carpet or the introduction of screens and internal walls can all have a noticeable effect on the acoustics of a church. Early consultation will enable the Adviser to work with the parish towards a common end, avoiding the confrontation which may result when a parish, having committed itself to an inappropriate course of action, refuses to be dissuaded by the Adviser. If the Adviser is unable to recommend the proposed work the Chancellor may, in serious cases, feel obliged to resolve the matter by a hearing in the Consistory Court.

Consultants

The employment of an independent organ consultant is normally helpful when a parish has received conflicting recommendations from different organ builders and needs disinterested advice at a more detailed level than the Diocesan Organs Adviser can give.

It must be appreciated that although the Diocesan Organs Adviser almost invariably gives free advice to a parish, his primary duty is to advise the Diocesan Advisory Committee. If a parish requires detailed, as opposed to general, advice it must expect to pay for it; but there is no reason why a Diocesan Organs Adviser should not be invited to serve in this capacity, which should not raise any problems of divided loyalties for him, as between the parish and the Diocesan Advisory Committee.

There are really two kinds of consultancy. The first amounts to an inspection of the situation, the consideration of alternative approaches and the recommendation of one builder or scheme of work rather than another. The second is closer to the role of an architect, inspecting work in progress and certifying progress as well as working with the organ builder at a considerable level of detail. The first is normally remunerated by a set fee, the second by a percentage of the organ builder's price.

It is essential that a consultant should have a thorough understanding of the principles of organ building and, where historic instruments are concerned, a wide experience of the historical development of the British organ. On occasion distinguished musicians with a limited knowledge of organ building have recommended schemes which, in the particular circumstances of the case, were either incapable of satisfactory execution or unreasonably costly to achieve.

VIII ORGAN BUILDERS

Choice

In recent years there has been a tendency to place contracts abroad, possibly because it is felt that only there can a first-class classical instrument be obtained. Quite apart from the question whether such instruments are suitable for accompanying the Anglican liturgy, it is fair to point out that nowadays several British organ builders have acquired European training and experience, and are able to build first-class classical organs with tracker action and well-designed tonal schemes.

It is not possible to categorise British organ builders neatly. They differ in type and style of work in which they are proficient, and the smaller firms also vary considerably in standards and consequently in price. Some builders, generally the larger firms, can undertake almost any type of work. The smaller ones specialize, sometimes in the design and building of small organs exclusively, though more often in tuning and jobbing repairs with restricted skills to match. Parishes should beware equally of the builder who seeks to do more work than is really necessary and, on the other hand, of the one who claims to do the work for half the price of his rivals, and who in fact is only going to do half the job.

Parishes will naturally wish to be satisfied that the firm they employ is reliable and trustworthy. Any organ-building firm worthy of the name should have an established workshop, employ full-time trained staff, and be ready to demonstrate examples of the type of work for which it submits estimates. It should also be financially stable in order to maintain the authenticity of guarantees. Part-time organ builders should not normally be employed. Repairs by amateurs have almost always proved disastrous; however well-meaning and initially attractive such offers may be, they should be declined.

Estimates

Some parishes invite estimates from several builders as a matter of course. This is not really helpful for the parish and less than fair to the organ builders, since the production of estimates is genuinely costly in

13

time and money. Some firms quite reasonably charge a nominal fee for this service. The fee is usually remitted if a contract is placed with the organ builder in question. The parish should be serious in its intention and make this clear from the outset.

No more than three estimates should be necessary for work expected to cost above £5,000. Work of £5,000 or less need have only one or two estimates at most. Work below £1,000 may reasonably be placed without competition to the firm which has the care of the instrument, provided the parish are satisfied with its services.

Competitive estimates are of little value unless obtained from firms of comparable quality of workmanship. The evaluation of tenders is not assisted by the invitation of complicated estimates with many supplementaries. It is better to invite tenders for a basic scheme and go into details later with the firm that is selected. Care should be taken to see that estimates are comprehensive, taking into account additional charges such as accommodation, transport and tax.

Estimates should be submitted in writing with at least one copy. Acceptance by the parish should be confirmed in writing, with an assurance that a faculty or archdeacon's certificate has been obtained.

IX CARE AND MAINTENANCE

If an organ is properly cared for it will last longer and cost less in the long run. Unreliability or discomfort to the player will give warning that an overhaul is becoming necessary. A contract with an organ builder for regular tuning and attention to minor faults is essential. The organist can do much to maintain the condition and value of the instrument by drawing the tuner's attention to such faults. The tuner should provide a log book for this purpose and note and date the attention given. The blowing plant is not the responsibility of the organ builder, and should be regularly oiled and checked by a qualified engineer or blower manufacturer.

X HEATING AND VENTILATION

The heating and ventilation of the church and organ surroundings are of first importance. Extremes of damp and dryness are inimical to the long life and proper functioning of an organ.

An organ builder should invariably be consulted before any alteration is made to an existing heating system or before a new one is installed. Instances have been known of the outlet vent of a hot air system being placed underneath the organ or directly opposite and pointing at it, and have proved expensively disastrous. Humidifying systems may be a palliative in such cases, but it is important to tackle the trouble at source.

Fuller information is contained in a leaflet *Damage to organs through heating and abnormal and atmospheric conditions* published by the Federation of Master Organ Builders, of which copies may be obtained from the Council for the Care of Churches.

In view of the peculiar fire risks attaching to organs, all electric light and power wiring should be subject to periodic inspection and conform to the standards laid down by the Council in *Lighting and Wiring of Churches,* obtainable from the Council for the Care of Churches.

XI LEGAL ASPECTS

All work in Anglican churches is governed by the faculty jurisdiction, and application must be made through the Diocesan Registry to the Chancellor for a faculty to sanction, amongst other things, the introduction, alteration or disposal of any object. Thus a faculty will be required for the installation of an organ, whether new or secondhand, for alteration to the action, the tonal scheme or the case of an existing organ, or for the removal of the existing organ from the church. It will also be required for the removal of an organ from one part of the church to another.

In most dioceses lesser matters are delegated to archdeacons, who can authorise work by certificates, also obtainable by application through the Diocesan Registry. These cover such works as the cleaning and overhaul of the organ (without alteration) or the provision of a new blower. All applications for faculties and archdeacons' certificates are subject to the advice of the Diocesan Advisory Committee. Work put in hand without proper authorisation may result in penalties for the organ builder and his client. Advice on faculties and archdeacons' certificates can be obtained from the Diocesan Registry.

XII FINANCE

The organ is likely to be the most expensive item in any church, and its complex mechanism requires regular professional care and maintenance if it is to provide music for the liturgy without deficiency. But even with proper maintenance organs need to be cleaned and overhauled or more thoroughly repaired from time to time, the frequency depending largely upon the type of action and amount of use. It therefore makes practical sense to establish an organ fund separate from the general parish accounts so that there is a foundation on which to build when a large sum of money suddenly has to be raised. Such funds can be invested to increase their capital value. For the restoration of a historic organ it is possible that grants may be available towards the cost of the work, and enquiries should be addressed to the Organs Advisory Committee, Council for the Care of Churches, 83 London Wall, London EC2M 5NA.

XIII INSURANCE

As a result of discussions between the Ecclesiastical Insurance Office, the Council for the Care of Churches and the Federation of Master Organ Builders, it is suggested that organs in churches should be insured against 'loss or damage due to any accident or misfortune'. Particulars may be obtained from The Ecclesiastical Insurance Office plc, Beaufort House, Brunswick Road, Gloucester, GL1 1JZ.

APPENDIX A

Parishes may find useful the following particulars of other bodies with interests in church organs.

British Institute of Organ Studies

The British Institute of Organ Studies (BIOS) is a registered charity which exists to promote the preservation and appreciation of all that is best in British organ building, past and present.

BIOS can offer advice to parishes upon the restoration of historic organs, based upon a careful survey of the instrument itself, and consultation of a wide range of documentary material (some of it in the Institute's Archive). If a parish is uncertain about the historical and musical value of its organ, the Institute will be prepared to offer an opinion.

For the parish seeking to replace an unsatisfactory organ, it may be worth consulting BIOS' Redundant Organs Officer, who keeps a list of worthy organs in need of new homes.

Enquiries should be addressed to the Hon. Secretary, Dr Nicholas Thistlethwaite, Flat E, Newnham Cottage, Queen's Road, Cambridge, CB3 9AH.

Federation of Master Organ Builders

The purpose and objects of the Federation are:
To preserve and maintain the supremacy of British Organ Building throughout the world, to encourage and safeguard the artistic side of the craft by improving and elevating the status of those engaged therein either as employers or employees, and generally to further and protect the welfare and interests of its members.
The general adoption of equitable conditions of contract, including method of payment and all like questions.
The interchange of information and, when desirable, co-operation with other kindred societies throughout the country, and the collection and circulation of statistics of general interest to the trade.
To watch over all measures, legislative or otherwise, which are calculated to affect the interests of the organ building trade.

Any person or company, proprietary or limited, carrying on the trade of organ building in the British Isles is eligible to apply for membership.

The Federation conducts its business through an Executive Board. The members of the Federation hold an Annual Meeting as early as possible in each year at which the Board for the current year is elected. Enquiries should be addressed to the Secretary, Federation of Master Organ Builders, Petersfield, Hampshire, GU32 3AT.

Incorporated Society of Organ Builders

The objects for which the Society is established are:

To advance the science and practice of organ building, by discussion, inquiry, research, experiment, and other means and to diffuse knowledge regarding organ building by means of lectures, publications, exchange of information, and otherwise.

To provide a central organisation for organ builders, and generally to do all such things as from time to time may be necessary to elevate the status, and procure the advancement of the interests of the profession.

To provide for the better definition and protection of the profession by a system of examination and the issue of certificates and distinctions, and to institute and establish scholarships, grants, rewards and other benefactions.

The members of the Society consist of five classes, viz. Students, Ordinary Members, Associates, Fellows and Councillors.

An Ordinary Member has recognised training in the craft of organ building, five years practical experience (excluding a period of recognised training), is sponsored by two members of the Society (other than Students), holds a recognised Certificate of Competence in the craft or has passed such examination or examinations as the Council may determine, and is accepted by the Council as an Ordinary Member. Associates must have ten years practical experience. Fellows must hold a position of authority in the craft and have fifteen years practical experience. Councillors fail to qualify as any of the foregoing, but must have held a position of responsibility in the craft for more than ten years. The President and Vice-President are elected from Fellows of the Council. Enquiries should be addressed to the Secretary, Incorporated Society of Organ Builders, Petersfield, Hampshire, GU32 3AT.

Royal College of Organists

The Royal College of Organists, founded in 1864, was incorporated by Royal Charter in 1893, with a Supplemental Charter granted in 1966. The College's objects include the maintenance of a library and the provision of a central organisation in London where information on organs is available to any persons requiring it. The Library contains an unrivalled collection of reference books on the history of the organ and its design and construction, together with many descriptions and specifications of particular organs in churches throughout the British Isles. Enquiries should be addressed to the Royal College of Organists, Kensington Gore, London, SW7 2QS.

Royal School of Church Music

The Royal School of Church Music is pleased to give advice on any matters which concern organs in churches, whatever denomination they may be. As far as Anglican churches are concerned this advice would always be in deference to the views of the Diocesan Organs Adviser, who should always be the first person to be approached.

When problems arise as a result of liturgical rearrangement, where the siting of a choir, organ and organist is of vital importance, it may be possible for one of the RSCM Commissioners to pay a call when he is in the area, and visit the church in question.

Many smaller points can be cleared up and assistance given by correspondence, and churches are asked to write to the Director, RSCM, Addington Palace, Croydon, CR5 9AD, when in need of any help or advice concerning the organ and its place in worship today.

APPENDIX B

Select Reading List For Detailed Study

Blanton, J.E. *The Organ in Church Design* (Albany, Texas, 1958)
  The Revival of the Organ Case (Albany, Texas, 1967)

Clutton, C. and Niland, A. *The British Organ* (London, 1963, 2nd revised edition, 1982)

Langwill, L. and Boston, N. *Church and Chamber Barrel Organs* (Edinburgh, 1966)

Niland, A. *Introduction to the Organ* (London, 1968)

Norman, H. and H.J. *The Organ Today* (London, 1966, 2nd edition, 1981)

Norman, J. *The Organs of Britain, An Appreciation and Gazetteer* (Newton Abbot, 1984)

Sumner, W.L. *The Organ, Its Evolution, Principles of Construction and Use* (London, 1952, 5th edition, 1975)

Williams, P. *A New History of the Organ, from the Greeks to the Present Day* (London, 1980)

Wilson, M. *The English Chamber Organ* (Oxford, 1968)